WALKS

WALKS IN DORSET

G. H. OSBORN

For the Dorset Rights of Way Group (Ramblers Association)

SPURBOOKS LIMITED

Published by:
SPURBOOKS LIMITED
1 Station Road
Bourne End
Buckinghamshire

S B N O 902875 83 3

Printed by Maund & Irvine Ltd., Tring, Herts.

Index

INTRODUCTION

OF ALL the counties in this lovely country, Dorset must surely be placed amongst the fairest. It has everything to delight the eye and uplift the mind. A magnificent rugged coastline unrivalled for beauty in Europe. Snug harbours and coves. Miles of gently sloping golden beaches bordered by the wild heath, known as Egden Heath, so beloved by Thomas Hardy. Behind lie the the great rolling chalk hills hiding in their folds the ancient and beautiful villages seemingly sleeping, whilst the summits are crowned by the great hill-forts built before the dawn of history by the Iron-Age folks who made their homes in this most ancient part of England.

Dorset is still the least populated county of England and the least built over. It has no coast road for motors to thunder along and the only town of any size, Poole, is tucked away in the extreme south-east of the county.

Apart from Poole, there are few towns and all of them small. Small they may be, but each of them has a beauty all of its own and a history which is part of the very fabric of England. Dorchester, built by the Romans and still bearing their imprint. Sherborne with a lovely Abbey and School. Shaftesbury the highest town in England sitting proudly on the hill top overlooking the glorious Blackmoor Vale. Wimborne with its great Minster nestling by the Stour gliding through green meadows. Wareham, the walled town virtually unchanged since Saxon times. Lyme Regis, so beloved of Jane Austen, with the tiny harbour at the foot of a steep hill. Blandford the fairest Georgian town in all England.

The Castles and Abbeys of Dorset are few, but they rank with the finest in the land. Who can look unmoved by the ruins of the great Castle at Corfe, or not be transported back in time when looking at the best preserved Abbey in England at Milton Abbas or at that other gem of Medieval England the beautiful Abbey Church at Sherborne?

In so rural and beautiful a county, well provided with footpaths, the number of walks through scenes of great beauty and interest must run into hundreds.

Obviously to compile a complete list of such walks is not practical and so the Author has had to face up to the difficult task of selecting some twenty-four walks, divided amongst five divisions of the county, each covering, it is hoped, some different aspect of the beauty of this lovely shire.

Each of the walks has been carefully selected to give an example of that part of the county and every inch has been walked by the Author. Wherever it was thought there might be some confusion great care has been taken to give explicit instructions.

The length of the walks has been kept to an average length of about five miles to give time to stroll along looking at the beauty all around and time to visit an object of interest in the neighbourhood of the walk. This is not a book for the hardened walker who merely wants to cover a lot of miles each day; it is a book for holiday makers, retired people, nature lovers, people with young children, and the not too active who just want to get out for a day enjoying the fresh air and the beauty of the countryside.

Not many years ago most books on walks would suggest taking a train to some point, walking in a straight line and then taking a bus or a train back to the starting point. Today this is all changed, countryside railways have closed, buses become far and few between. On the other hand, personal transport has become almost universal and so these walks have been based on starting at some convenient point and walking in a circle to return to your car. Wherever possible places where refreshments may be obtained are given and since these walks have been planned to allow plenty of time wherever something of interest is encountered, a few notes are given to enable a visit.

Very few of the walks are particularly strenuous but due to the nature of the countryside many are hilly and involve some up-hill work. Frequently the paths are narrow, through fields overgrown with brambles and nettles and often the grass is long and wet after rain and the heath abounds with boggy soil. For the purpose of these walks, therefore, the Author recommends waterproof boots or shoes and advises the ladies to wear trousers.

All walkers are advised to take with them the 1.25000 Ordnance Maps which add so much pleasure to any walk. Please remember to close all the gates behind you and to take home with you any paper or tins and anything else resulting from a picnic.

The Ramblers Association and the Dorset Rights of Way Group have done work beyond praise in protecting the footpaths of the county. Indeed without their efforts these walks would not have been possible.

It should always be remembered that the greater part of these walks cross land owned by farmers and every care should be taken to protect their interests. The average Dorset Farmer is a responsible person willing to co-operate provided the walker behaves in a similar responsible way.

All the walks have been made along paths designated as official footpaths on the Definitive Footpath Map to be seen at County Hall but it should be borne in mind that deviation orders may be made from time to time and there may be slight differences in the route. If this does happen the new path will be shown on the map at the County Hall.

My thanks are due to the Dorset section of the Ramblers Association who gave me the opportunity to write up these walks and especially to that tireless worker of the rights of pedestrians, Mrs Ruth Colyer for encouragement. Last and certainly not least the Author would also like to thank his secretary Mrs Elizabeth Lane who put in much time and care in the planning of these walks.

Finally, it only remains for the Author to wish the reader many happy hours of gentle walking along the paths outlined in this book.

The Isle of Purbeck

"FAIR Purbeck which nowhere has her peere" wrote Drayton the poet nearly four hundred years ago and the saying is as true today as it was then.

Only fifteen miles in length and eight in width at its maximum, it is still unspoilt. It has no town of any size but it is the villages nestling in the folds of the great hills which do so much to make Purbeck the perfect synthesis of natural and man-made beauty. In the lovely villages all the houses are made of the gracious light grey Purbeck stone even to the roofs. Time has mellowed the buildings and festooned them with multi-coloured lichens so that they fit perfectly into the countryside.

Purbeck is, of course, only an isle by courtesy because today a cause-way links it to the mainland at Wareham. Yet because main roads are few and paths across the springy turf on the hills are frequent, one can in a few minutes be high up where the only sound is that of the sky-lark or the shrill shriek of the gull hovering over the restless sea as it laps the great cliffs of Purbeck.

Here then, on sunny days at almost any time of the year some of the finest walks in all England are freely available.

Erratum

The map on page 13 for Walk 1 is incorrect. Please use this map. The error will be corrected in future editions.

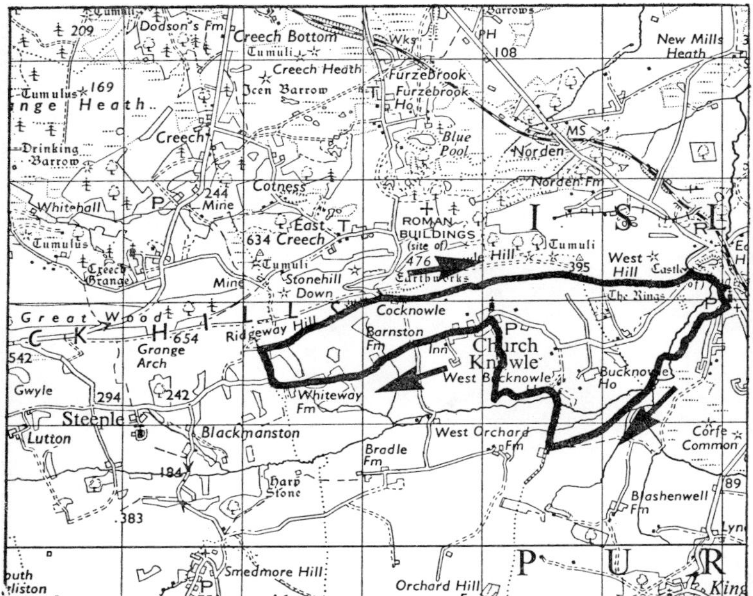

Corfe Castle

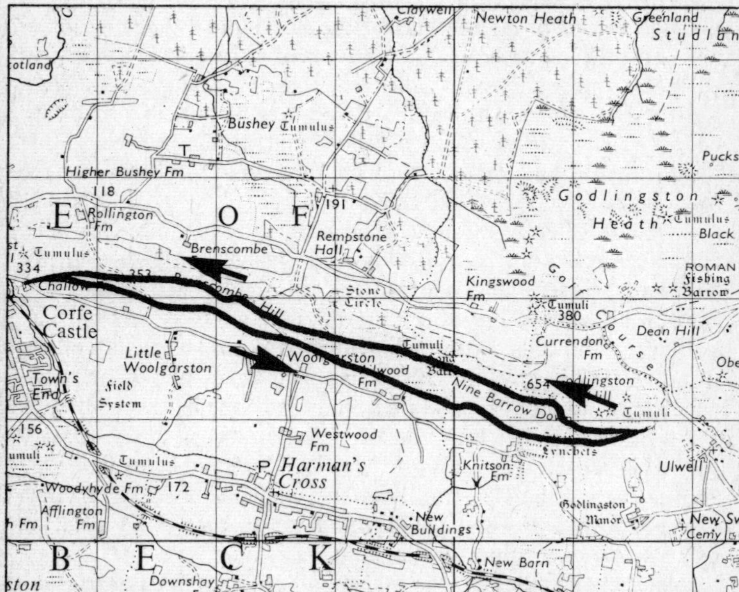

Crown Copyright — Scale: 1 inch = 1 mile

Church Knowle, Corfe Castle

Distance: 5 miles.
Walking time: 3 hours approximately.
Degree of difficulty: This walk is only for the reasonably active as there are several gates to be climbed and a fairly steep ascent of Ridgeway Hill. Ladies are advised to wear trousers.
Ordnance map: Purbeck Sheet SY 87/97/SZ. 07 1.25000.

LEAVE car in car park just off West Street. This is clearly marked. At the opposite end of the car park is a stile with a yellow mark on it. Cross this and continue along the hedge following line of telegraph posts. After a while you will reach a patch of overgrown track with paths going right and left. Take the right hand path until you reach a stile with a yellow marker, and an open field. On your right hand side you will see Bucknowle House. Continue on over old stone bridge until you come directly in front of West Bucknowle House.

Here care must be taken as it is easy to lose the way. Cross the stile and keeping the iron gate to your left continue on through the field. At the end of the field you will see a ruined house on the hill. About fifty yards below this in the wood you will see a stile with yellow marker. Cross this and go on through a patch overgrown with nettles. Cross field by side of stream until you reach a bridge with a yellow marker. Do *not* cross this but turn right and go to top of field (left hand corner). Here a track leads directly to Church Knowle.

At Church Knowle follow main road to left for about a mile, passing Barnston Cross Roads and Barnston Farm. Shortly afterwards on left hand side you will see a small farm, Whiteway Farm, and almost opposite this on right hand side is a track leading to the hills. After 200 yards you will see a boundary stone, turn left here for 100 yards and then follow the track which leads to the right and on to the top of the hill.

From the top the track can very easily be seen and is mainly down hill all the way to Corfe Castle. The view from the ridge above Corfe Castle overlooking the whole of Poole Harbour, Corfe Castle and village, Church Knowle and the Purbecks, must be one of the finest in England.

When the track meets the main road at Corfe Castle continue along until you reach the foot of the mound on which the Castle is built. There is small path here to the right which will lead you directly to the Square and West Street.

Places of interest on route.

Corfe Castle: The Castle and Village are well worth exploring.

Church Knowle: A very beautiful Church.

Barnestone Manor: Saxon Manor house rebuilt and fortified by Normans. Open to the public in summer on Wednesday 2-6 p.m.

Refreshments:

Corfe Castle: Several good public houses and restaurants around the Square.

Church Knowle: The New Inn serves very good snacks at bar.

Dean Hill

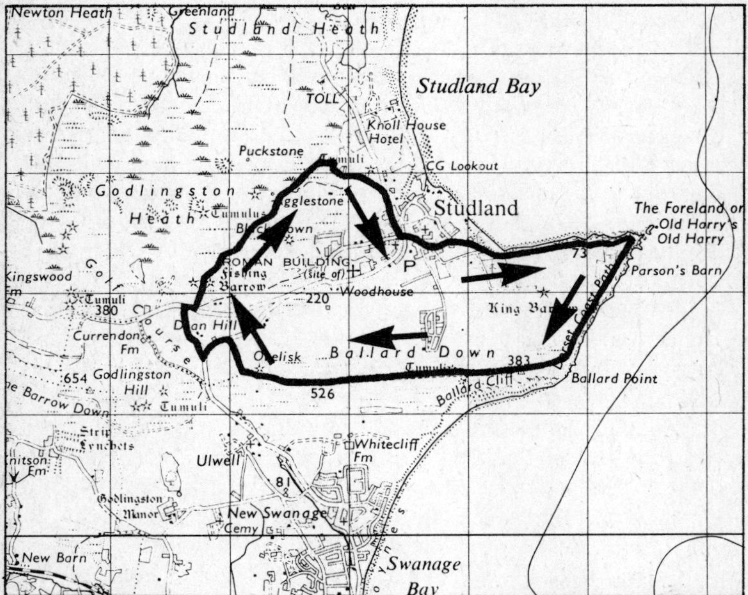

Crown Copyright Scale: 1 inch = 1 mile

Agglestone, Studland, Ballard Down, Dean Hill

Distance: 6 miles.
Walking time: 3 hours approximately.
Degree of difficulty: Very easy walking involving some up-hill sections. Trousers advised for Ladies.
Ordnance map: Purbeck Sheet SY 87/97/SZ 07. 1.25000.

FROM Corfe Castle take the car along the road to Studland, for about 4 miles. At this point you will see the Golf Club and car park on left hand side. Continue on round the bend in the road and you will come to a parking space with a sign post saying "Footpath to Agglestone."

Follow path and shortly afterwards you will see on the right hand side a further sign post to "The Agglestone". Continue across the Heath on this path until you reach the Agglestone itself. This huge rock of Ferruginous Sandstone is 18 ft. high, 80 ft. round and weighs 400 tons and is all that is left possibly of a layer of sandstone that once covered all this heathland and has been eroded by time and weather. The views over the harbour and sea are superb.

The footpath continues on past the Agglestone. It is very narrow but it is essential to keep closely to it as in wet weather the Heath is very boggy. After a few hundred yards the path meets a main track. Turn right here and continue on bearing to right. Shortly you will meet the main Poole-Studland road just before it enters the village. You will have to follow this road for a few hundred yards until you reach a sign post saying "To Banks Arms". Do not take the road just previous which says "To Beach".

Continuing along this road you will find the Manor House facing you. At this point turn right, pass the "Banks Arms" and continue on down the hill. At the bottom take the path to the left which leads to cliff walk.

Continue along until you reach Handfast Point and then continue on the cliff path until you reach Ballard Point. Here the path turns inland and you will find yourself walking over Ballard Down, one of the most beautiful places in England.

Continue until you reach an obelisk. A few yards farther on the footpath turns right and down hill until it reaches the Swanage-Studland road. Turn left here and walk along the road for a few hundred yards until you see a stile on your right hand side. Cross this and follow the path diagonally across the field to where you can see another stile. After this stile the path continues upward until you emerge on to the golf course.

There is a right of way across the Course, continue in a straight line i.e. due north across the course to the hedge on the farther side in which you will see a gate. This takes you directly on to the Corfe-Studland road and the car park is a few yards to the right.

Note: There may be other walks in England to equal the beauty of this one but none can surpass it. On a lovely day the view from Ballard Down of the Heath, the coast from Anvil Point to

St. Catherines on the Isle of Wight and the blue sea lapping the chalk cliffs can leave no one unmoved.

Places of interest on route.

Studland: Often called the incomparable. A beautiful village at the foot of the Purbecks with a beach of miles of golden sands and shallow waters. Ideal for children. The Church, a beautiful example of Norman building should not be missed. See also the remains of the Saxon cross in the lane just pass the "Banks Arms".

Refreshments: Snacks and drinks may be obtained at the "Banks Arms" at Studland (about halfway) which has an outdoor terrace overlooking the sea. On a fine day, however, a picnic high up on the cliffs overlooking "Old Harry" can be recommended. Here the views are beautiful beyond description and the peace is only broken by the wheeling sea-gulls over the nearby rocks.

WALK 3

Kimmeridge

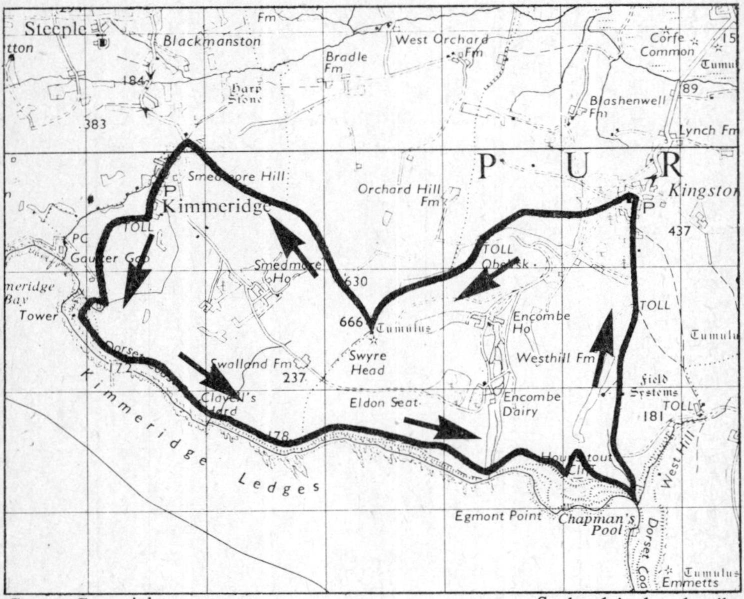

Crown Copyright | Scale: 1 inch = 1 mile

Chapmans Pool, Swyre Head, Kimmeridge

Distance: 9 miles.
Walking time: 5 hours approximately.
Degree of difficulty: This walk, one of the finest in England is very undulating involving considerable climbing. A great deal of the way is along a narrow cliff path unfenced and at times only three feet wide with a drop of several hundred feet. Not advised, therefore, for children, animals, elderly people or those with a fear of heights.
Ordnance map: Purbeck 87/97 SZ07. 1.25000.
Starting point: Small telephone exchange at top of hill leading down to Kimmeridge. Map ref. 91.9/80.2.

LEAVE car at telephone exchange. There is an old quarry here which is ideal for parking. Follow road down to the harbour. Just before you reach the cove you will see a path on the left hand side going up towards a monument.

The path is very clear and continues on for three miles to Chapmans Pool. The path is very easy to follow but the section on Hounds Tout cliff up to Egmont Point is very steep as is also the descent on the other side down to Chapmans Pool.

From Chapmans Pool the path back to Kingston is very clearly marked. It is a mile and a half long climbing all the way but a very easy gradient.

At Kingston continue on past the "Scott Arms" and church for about a mile. There you will see a sign post "Swyre Head". Pass through a gate and follow the well defined footpath right up to the tumulus on the top of Swyre Head. From this point there is a panoramic view of great beauty.

Here take the well marked path going north-west from the tumulus. It continues in a straight line along the ridge above Smedmore House and finally descends to the telephone exchange where your car is parked.

Note: This is the longest walk recommended in this book but is one of outstanding beauty. The views in all directions are superb fully equal to that of Ballard Down.

Places of interest on route.

Kimmeridge: The cove and small fishing port is very picturesque. Many fossils can be found here on the beach.

Encombe House: From the tumulus on Swyre Head you will see below you to the north Encombe House and estate. Seat of the Eldon family but only open to the public on rare occasions.

Smedmore House: On the way home on the upper ridgeway you will see Smedmore House to your left below you. The house is 16th century with 17th century front set in 50 acres and is the home of the Clavell Family. Open to the public on Wednesday afternoons June to September.

Refreshments. Advisable to take your own and picnic on the turf overlooking the sea. Good snacks are obtainable at the "Scott Arms" in Kingston.

South Dorset: A region of wild seascape, rolling hills, immense panoramic views, small towns and charming villages. As one walks the strong sea air fills ones lungs and the joy of living is ever present. There are few towns but the villages built of the local stone are full of interest and wholly satisfying to the eye.

South Dorset

A region of wild seascape, rolling hills, immense panoramic views, small towns and charming villages. As one walks the strong sea air fills ones lungs and the joy of living is ever present. There are few towns but the villages built of the local stone are full of interest and wholly satisfying to the eye.

WALK 4

Hardy Memorial

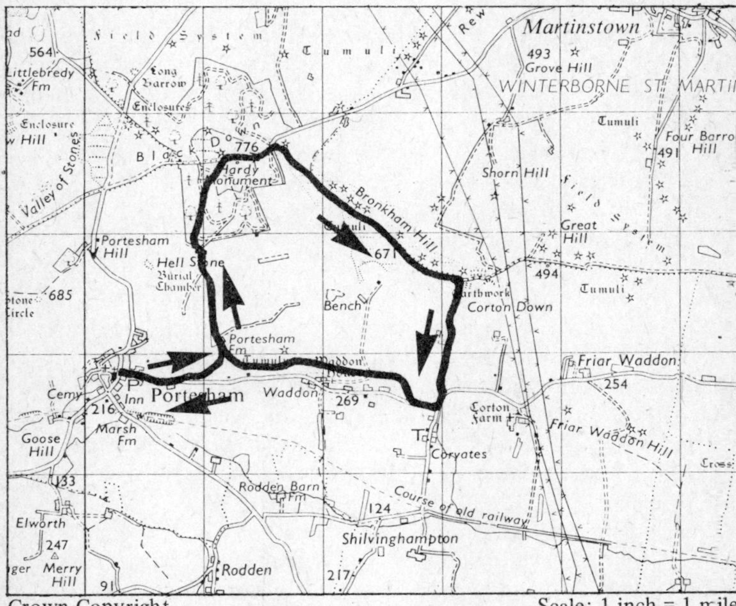

Crown Copyright

Scale: 1 inch = 1 mile

Portesham, Hardy Memorial

Distance: 5 miles.
Walking time: 2 hours.
Degree of difficulty: Easy walking.
Ordnance map: Weymouth North. SY/68/78. 1.25000.
Starting point: Hardy memorial. Map ref. 87.6/61.2.

LEAVE your car at the large car park provided at the Hardy memorial. Return to main road and turn right i.e. east down hill. A few yards down the road is a small car park and opposite a bridle path sign. Take this path which leads all along the ridge for about one and a half miles when near the tumuli there is a path branching off main track to south. This will take you around the base of Corton Hill and on to main road.

Turn westward here and walk along main road for about a hundred yards. Here there is a path going up the hill and above little Wadden Farm and Wadden House. Continue on until you reach Portesham Farm from whence it is downhill all the way into Portesham.

For the return go back as far as Portisham Farm but turn left at the farm and follow the track past Black Down Barn and leave the wood on your right hand side. The track now leads directly to the memorial and your car.

Note: A pleasant easy walk with superb views over Lyme Bay and the Chesil Bank.

Places of interest on route.

Hardy Memorial: Tower erected to the memory of Admiral Sir Thomas Hardy whose home was at Portisham. He was at Trafalgar and Nelson died in his arms. The tower is in a dangerous condition and ascent is no longer possible.

Hellstone: In a field a hundred yards due west of Black Down Barn is the pre-historic megalith or burial place. Nine upright stones support a capstone 10 ft. long. One of the finest examples in England.

Portesham: Very charming village built of a lovely light grey stone. Many charming houses. The church is well worth a visit.

Refreshments. Good snacks obtainable at the Kings Arms Hotel at Portesham.

Littlebredy

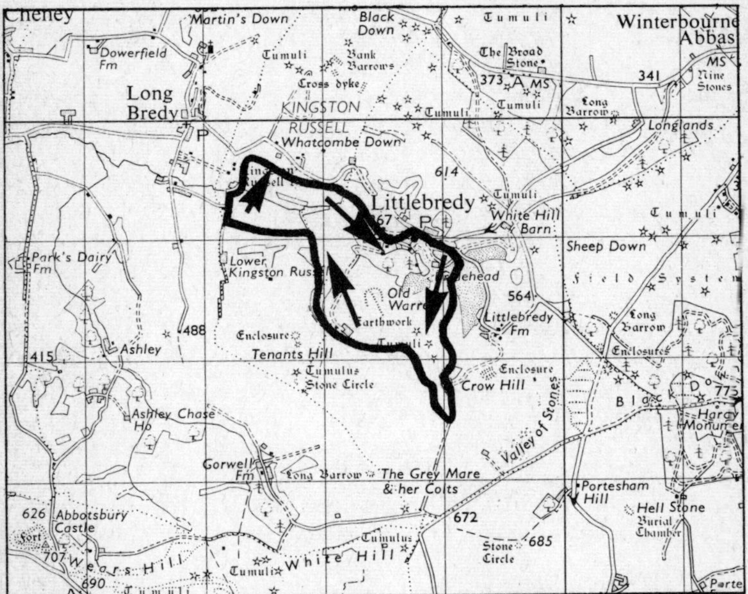

Crown Copyright Scale: 1 inch = 1 mile

Littlebredy, Kingston Russell, Littlebredy

Distance: 7 miles.
Time: 3 hours.
Degree of difficulty: Easy walking.
Ordnance map: SY. 58. Abbotsbury.
Starting point: Littlebredy (approximately 6 miles SW of Dorchester). Map reference 89/59 Abbotsbury.

LEAVE car in middle of village. Take the path eastwards past the big house Bridehead which is on your right hand side. Just past the entrance to Bridehead you will see a gate leading into a cricket field. Pass through the gate and continue on path which leads along the side of the hill. Continue on until you reach some farm buildings, Topparts Dairy, immediately beyond which is a small pit. At this point turn and follow path which goes back the other side of the hill.

The path leads down between the hills until you come to some farm buildings, Foxholes Farm. Immediately before entering farm yard is a gate on your left hand side. Go through this then up the hill a few yards and then turn right and follow path leaving the coppice on your right hand side. Near the end of the coppice the path goes diagonally across the field in N.W. direction. Follow along through the fields until you reach the next coppice. Half way along is a gap through which the path goes. Continue on until you reach the road near the farm buildings called Lower Kingston Russell Farm.

Follow the road due north to the ford where you will see an old stone house. The path goes directly across the front of this and along a grass path through a gate at the side of the garden. Just before the grass path narrows to an earth track you will see a gate on your right hand side. Go through gate and continue on across the fields through various gates you will see. These paths will take you directly to Littlebredy.

Note: A walk of great beauty and interest. Best walked in dry weather.

Refreshments: None available on this route. Snacks etc. easily available in nearby villages such as Portisham.

Places of interest on route.

Bridehead: Lovely old house by side of lake from which arises the tiny stream, the Bride, which makes its way to Burton Bradstock.

Kingston Russell House: An imposing stately home built by John Russell founder of one of the greatest families in England.

Strip Lynchetts: On many of the fields on the sides of hills you will see on this walk there are what appear to be grass terraces. These Celtic Fields or Strip Lynchetts were made originally by Neolithic man when he first farmed the hill tops. To prevent the loss of top soil by rain fall all the strips were terraced.

Broadmayne

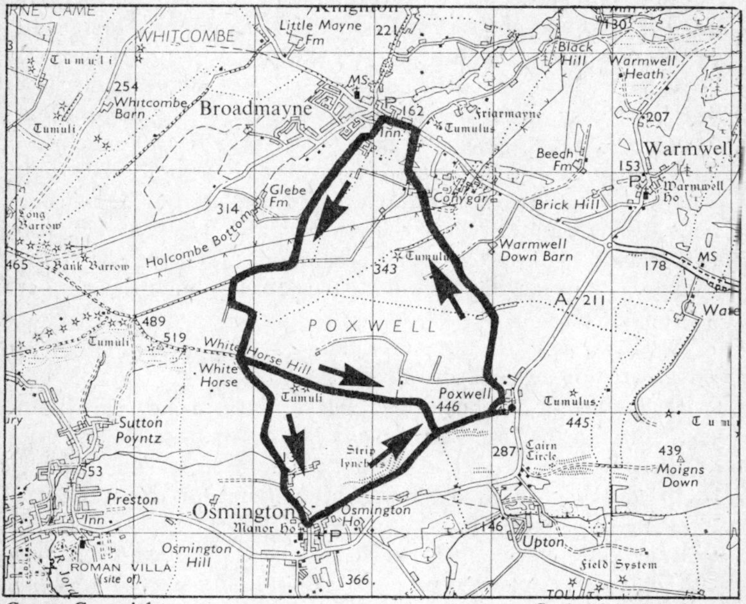

Scale: 1 inch = 1 mile

Poxwell, Broadmayne

Distance: about 6 miles.
Walking time: 3 hours approximately.
Degree of difficulty. Fairly easy walking in dry weather. After rain it is a very muddy walk.
Ordnance Map: Weymouth (North) SY 68/78. 1.25000.
Starting point: The Post Office. Broadmayne. Map ref. 73.0./86.6.

THERE is a good car park at the "Black Dog Inn" which is only a few yards from the Post Office. The path is immediately at the side of the Post Office and goes past Broadmayne House. The path is wide and well defined being an ancient sheep drive. It continues until a gate to a field is reached from which the path can be seen going uphill.

At the top of the field there is a gate and once through you find yourself in a lane. Turn right and carry on past Half Moon Coppice. A few yards past the coppice the path diverges. Either path can be taken as they both lead to the track along the summit of White Horse Hill. If you take the left hand path it is well defined until you come to the ridge of White Horse Hill and is, of course, shorter than the path to the right.

As you walk eastwards along the ridge of White Horse Hill you have magnificent views over the coast and Weymouth Bay. Just below you is the carved figure of George III on horseback. After passing the White Horse you will see in front to your right a path leading down to Osmington. For the very fit a detour can be made here down to the village, which is worth a visit, and then back to Poxwell by the Old Roman road at the end of the village. This will add an hour to the journey but the detour is recommended.

For those who do not make this detour continue along the ridge until you descend into Poxwell.

At Poxwell just opposite the churchyard is a farm. The path goes through the farm and up the hill beyond until at the top you reach a field which has a path right across it left unploughed by the farmer. Follow this to the little coppice at the other side of the field.

Here you find yourself faced with rolling open fields but although a right of way, no clear path is to be seen. If possible use a hand compass because your path is almost due north. Continue on until you see a large wood in front of you. This is Warmwell Wood and your path is to the west of this down through Friar Mayne Farm and so to the main road where you turn left into Broadmayne.

Refreshments: At the "Black Dog" in Broadmayne excellent snacks may be obtained.

Places of interest on route.

Broadmayne: Small village with some nice old houses. The Church was relentlessly restored by the Victorians.

Poxwell: Surely one of the smallest hamlets in England. The Manor House is very beautiful and worth inspection.

White Horse: 323 ft. high and 280 ft. long this was carved out in

1815 to commemorate the visit of George III to Weymouth.
Note: This walk has something of everything. Smiling countryside, rolling hills and woods, and a trackway along the Ridgeway with unsurpassed views of the valley and the coastline. Do, however, try to take a pocket compass with you for the return section.

WALK 7

Abbotsbury

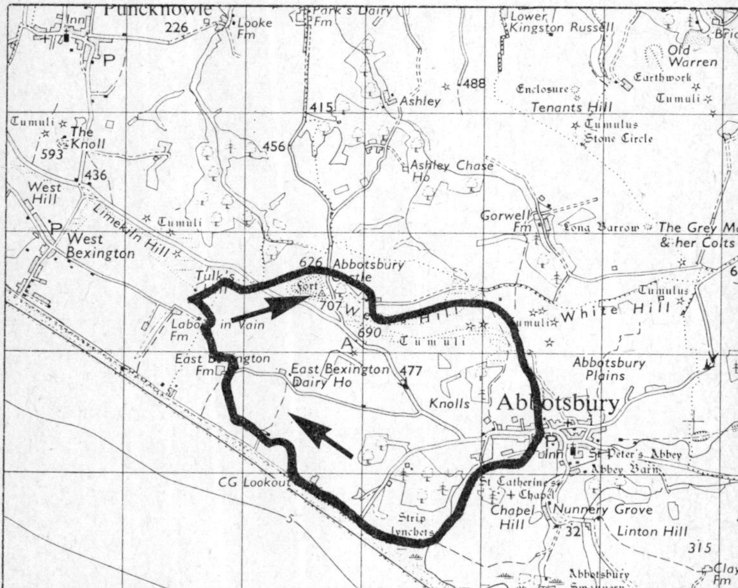

Scale: 1 inch = 1 mile

Distance: 5 miles.
Time: 2½ hours approximately.
Degree of difficulty: Easy walking but a climb of 700 ft. is involved.
Ordnance map: Abbotsbury SY58. 1.25000.
Starting point: Coastguard Lookout on Chesil Beach. Map ref. 84.9/55.4.

CARRY on past the Coastguards' hut for a 1000yds. Here there is a footpath on your right hand side leading up to East Bexington Farm. The path goes along the east side of East Bexington Farm then immediately behind it and across the fields in a north-westerly direction until it reaches the hedge at "Labour-in-Vain Farm." Here the path leaves the farmhouse to the left hand side and goes due north up the hill in a straight line until it reaches the road.

A few yards along the road will be seen a gateway into a field through which the path goes to Abbotsbury Castle. The path follows right round the base of the Iron-Age fort and then continues along the ridge of the hills having the sea on your right hand and Wears Farm on your left.

Continue along the ridge of the hill until you are roughly in line with St. Catherine's Chapel on a hill to your right. Here the path continues downward towards Abbotsbury Village which can be seen very clearly. The path goes to a wood, Jubilee Coppice, and then leaving this to the left, skirts the wood and reaches a path which goes directly into Abbotsbury Village.

From here the path to the Beach is clearly marked all the way. At the beach turn right and walk along until you reach the Coastguards hut.

Note: There is a climb of 700 ft. from sea-level to the hill ridge but the ascent is gradual. From the ridge at the point where you are level with St. Catherine's Chapel, the view must surely be one of the loveliest in all England. Just to see this alone would justify the walk.

Refreshments: There are plenty of tea-rooms in Abbotsbury in summer. Snacks obtainable at the "Swan Inn".

Places of interest on route.

Chesil Bank: 11 miles long it is some five hundred feet wide and is a vast breakwater compiled of countless millions of pebbles the size of which varies in a regular manner so that at one end the pebbles are all large and at the other all small. Fishermen landing in fog can tell exactly where they are by the size of the pebbles.

Abbotsbury: One of the most ancient villages in England and certainly a centre of the earliest Christian worship in Britain. Here for many centuries was a splendid monastery of which little save the lovely Abbey Barn and St. Catherine's Chapel remains. The church is a little gem and was the scene of a battle in the Civil War, marks of which are still to be seen in the pulpit. The village is full of lovely old houses. The Swannery, the largest in England covering over 25 acres, has a population of over 1000 swans and has been here beyond recorded history.

West Dorset

ONE of the greatest charms of Dorset is that although it is so small a county it can be divided into several divisions each completely different in scenery.

West Dorset is not only one of the loveliest parts of Dorset but one of the loveliest parts of England. It has a coast line of rugged beauty unequalled in Europe, inside of which lie tiny harbours of great charm and beauty such as Lyme Regis whilst the hinterland is composed of great green hills in whose folds lie lonely valleys and remote hamlets.

Here one can walk all day long under a cloudless sky amid the most glorious scenery and yet not see a living soul. Truly a beautiful, romantic and lovely countryside in which to wander.

WALK 8

Spyway

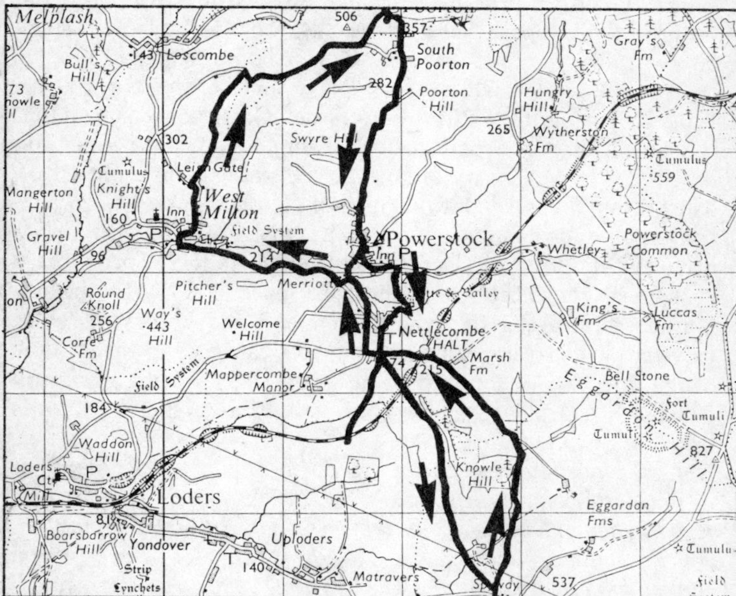

Crown Copyright

Scale: 1 inch = 1 mile

Powerstock, Spyway

Distance: 5 miles.
Time: 3 hours.
Degree of difficulty: Very easy walking.
Ordnance map: Maiden Newton. SY.59. 1.25000.
Starting point: Spyway (½ mile due north of Askerswell).
Map reference 93.2/53.0. A good car park at the Spyway Inn.

AT THE Spyway Inn follow road due west downhill for about 20 yards. Here there is a lane with a sign "Footpath to Powerstock". Follow this until you come to a farmhouse directly in front of you. Take the path to the right and follow on through the fields until you meet a road beyond a gate. Turn left here and follow the road past Powerstock Station.

Carry on to Nettlecoombe and the "Marquis of Lorne" which is the second turning on the right, opposite a gate leading to a farm. Immediately to the left hand side of the Inn is a footpath with a sign which leads directly to Powerstock.

For the return go down the road along which you came but do not take the path back to the "Marquis of Lorne". Instead continue five hundred yards until you come to a path on the right hand side which goes steeply uphill between overgrown hedges. This path goes past Powerstock Castle, of which all that remains is a motte and bailey. Continue downhill until you reach Castle Mill farm. Here take the path to the right which leads through the delightful hamlet of Nettlecoombe.

Continue on until you come to a signpost "Footpath to Spyway". Follow path across the fields to railway line where it is necessary to climb over the wire fence. Follow the clearly marked path along the edge of a wood and across the stiles between fields. Carry on as far as you can go and then follow hedge downhill to the right. This soon leads you to a path on which you started out. This point is only a few hundred yards from the Spyway Inn.

Note: A walk of great enchantment on a fine day. Probably at its finest in Spring or Autumn.

Refreshments: Surely one of the best areas for country inns, excellent snacks and meals at the "Spyway Inn". Good refreshments also obtainable at the "Marquis of Lorne" Nettlecoombe and the "Three Horseshoes" at Powerstock.

Places of interest on route.

Powerstock: One of the loveliest villages in the county. Subject of a B.B.C. documentary in 1970. The houses of honeygold stone cling around the village Church and give a picture of timeless peace. Do spare time to visit the church with its lovely Norman Chancel arch and 15th Century south door with the Madonna and Child still seeming to welcome all who come.

Powerstock Castle: Only the motte and bailey remain of the castle built by King John about 1200 A.D. Most of the walls were removed to build houses in Powerstock and surrounding villages. Only grass covered walls remain. A partial excavation was made in 1920 but a full scale excavation is still awaited.

Powerstock

West Milton, South Poorton, Powerstock

Distance: 5 miles.
Time: 2½ hours.
Degree of difficulty: Mildly strenuous.
Ordnance Map: Maiden Newton SY 59. 1.25000.
Starting Point: Powerstock. Map ref. 96.3/51.6.

LEAVE your car in the village. The "Three Horseshoes" where excellent snacks may be obtained, has a friendly landlord and good car park. Just opposite the church you will see a sign post "Bridle path to West Milton". Follow this path which is clearly marked. When you pass the gate into the last field before West Milton cross the field diagonally upwards towards the ruined church. There are a couple of stiles leading into the Churchyard.

When you reach the road outside the church turn right up the hill. Shortly afterwards you will see a sign on the right hand side "Bridle path to Poorton". This leads uphill but when, very soon you reach a lane beyond a gate, turn left and follow the lane all the way up the hill. At the top you find yourself in a field with a well defined path near the hedge. Continue on until you reach a Y junction. Take the left hand fork into field here and follow paths until after some fields you come to a small country lane. Turn right and continue until you come to "South Poorton".

In the centre of South Poorton, a hamlet so remote it is not mentioned in any guide book of the county, you will see a lane on the right hand side leading sharply downhill. This leads you to Bottom Farm. Continue along the road past the farm for about half a mile uphill where there is a singpost, "Private road only". Go along this road until you see a couple of houses both with gates bearing the sign "No Bridle Path". Take no notice of these as, of course, it is a recognised foot path.

Take the path past the front of the houses to your right. Just beyond is a gate which leads into a grass path going between hedges. Follow to the end and then carry on across a field to where you see a small thatched building. Turn right here and follow the lane directly to Powerstock.

Note: A very lovely walk through beautiful countryside. In wet weather it is advisable for ladies to wear trousers and water proof boots since in places near West Milton it is boggy.

Refreshments: "The Three Horseshoes" at Powerstock. Good snacks.

Places of interest on route.

Powerstock: One of the loveliest villages in the county.

West Milton, North Poorton, South Poorton: All very remote hamlets not mentioned in any guide book on the county. Nevertheless, some nice stone houses and worth visiting.

Lyme Regis

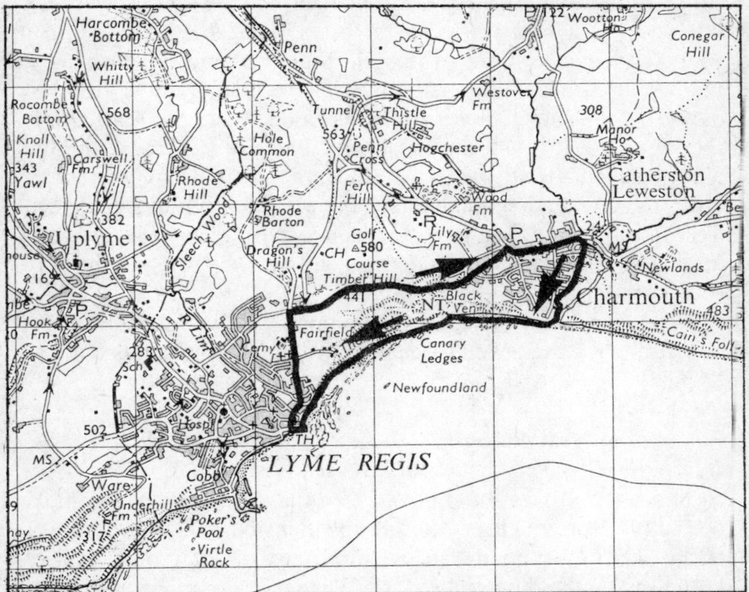

 Scale: 1 inch = 1 mile

Charmouth, Lyme Regis

Distance: 5 miles.
Walking time: 2½ hours.
Degree of difficulty: An easy walk.
Ordnance map: Axminster Sheet. SY29/39. 1.25000.
Note: This walk entails walking along the sea shore and the direction of the walk should be adjusted so that the tide is out when one reaches the shore. The footpath shown on the Ordnance map along the sea coast no longer exists, having slipped. In this description the walk is from Lyme Regis inland to Charmouth and along the shore from Charmouth to Lyme Regis but as suggested above the direction should be reversed according

to tide. Do not attempt the shore walk on an incoming tide since the tide comes in very fast.
Starting point: Axminster Sheet. SY 29/39. Map ref. 92.8./33.8.

LEAVE your car in the car park near the old church on the cliff. Walk back up the hill on the Charmouth Road for about a mile. This is a moderately steep section. Just past the first cross roads you meet is a sign on the right hand side indicating "Timber Hill", and a stile. Cross the style and continue on crossing a made up road. The path is well defined but somewhat overgrown. From the cliff top where one meets the golf course the views over Lyme and its lovely bay are superb. Continue along the path until near the fifteenth green where one must cross the course diagonally since the original path has collapsed over the cliff edge. The direction is, however, very clear and continuing over a stile the path leads gently downwards all the way to Charmouth.

Near the foot of the hill is a sign post, "to the Beach". Follow this and when the beach is reached walk along the sands back to Lyme.

Places of interest on route.
Lyme Regis: A very beautiful little sea port though very crowded in season. It was much loved by Jane Austen who used it as the setting for much of "Sense and Sensibility". The Cobb of 600ft. in length playing an essential part of the plot. The harbour was the landing place of the Duke of Monmouth of his ill-fated attempt to seize the crown of England.
Charmouth: Charming old town full of history. The "Queens Arms" was built by the last Abbot of Forde Abbey and was the scene of one of the most dramatic episodes in the escape of Charles II from Worcester.
Beach: The cliffs along the seashore from Charmouth to Lyme Regis are full of fossils and indeed the science of Palaeontology can be said to have been started here by the unearthing of an icthyosauras by a ten-year-old girl, Mary Anning in 1811.
Refreshments: At Lyme Regis all kinds may be obtained. The same is true at Charmouth but the walker requiring only simple snacks is especially recommended to "The George Inn" at the foot of the hill.

WALK 11

Symondsbury

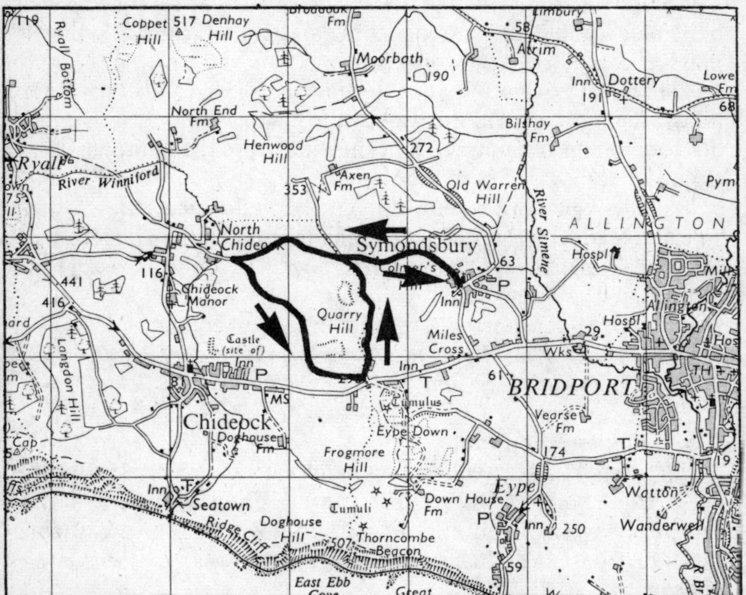

Scale: 1 inch = 1 mile

North Chideock, Quarry Hill, Symondsbury

Distance: 5 miles.
Walking time: 2 hours.
Degree of difficulty: Very easy walking.
Ordnance map: Bridport. SY 49 (and part of 48) 1.25000.
Starting point: Symondsbury. (1 mile N.W. Bridport) Map ref. 44.5/93.6.

LEAVE your car in the lane to the west of the church. Start walking up hill and continue up a gentle slope for about half a mile. At the Y junction keep left going up a hill. A little further on is a charming little pink cottage.

You will now find yourself walking through a gorge with high rocks on either side, a scene of some beauty. Carry on for about a further half mile when you will come to where four paths meet. This is Quarry Cross. Go down the lane to the left and follow this all the way to foot of the hill where a few cottages indicate that you are at North Chideock.

About 300 yards before the village you will see on the left hand side double gates. Cross these and continue along the well marked path over two further gates.

This takes you to the foot of Quarry Hill and you can either follow the path around the foot of the hill or climb right over the double summit of Quarry Hill. The view from the hill top is very beautiful at most times of the year.

Whether one goes round or over, the paths meet at the other side and lead straight to a gate which must be climbed. Here you will find yourself at Quarry Cross and it is only necessary to follow the track downhill to your car.

Note: A very pleasant walk through beautiful countryside.

Refreshments: The "Ilchester Arms" at Symondsbury provides simple but good snacks and liquid refreshment.

Places of interest on route.

Symondsbury: A very charming hamlet undeservedly left out of every guide book to Dorset. The church is well worth a visit and there are several lovely houses, but do not miss the row of cottages just past the "Ilchester Arms". Go to rear to see the full charm.

Lamberts Castle

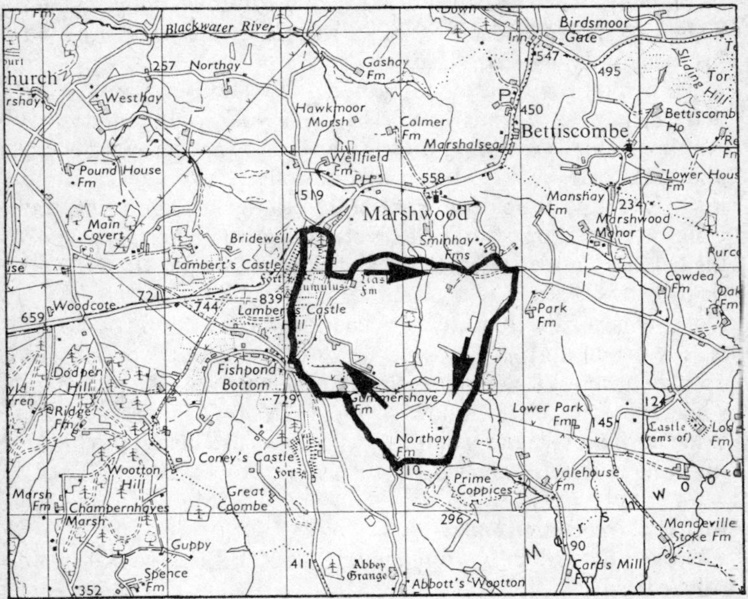

Crown Copyright

Scale: 1 inch = 1 mile

Marshwood Vale

Distance: 6 miles.
Walking time: 3 hours approximately.
Degree of difficulty: The actual walking is very easy but the walk should not be attempted after heavy rains as the blue lias becomes very boggy. In dry weather the ground is firm.
Ordnance map: Axminster sheet SY/29/39. 1.25000.

LEAVE the car at Peters Gore (map ref. 37-98.2). Immediately opposite you will see a sign "Lamberts Castle". Follow the path which will take you to the summit ridge of this Iron-Age fort. The views from the summit in all directions are amongst the finest in Dorset. The path here is very clear. Continue on and down through the Beech Grove at the other end. Walk a few yards along the road until you see a telephone box. Turn right here along a lane which runs along the base of Lamberts Castle.

After about five hundred yards you will see a sign to Nash Farm. There is a path down to it and at the north side there are three gates. Take the centre one which leads down between high hedges to a ford and up again on the other side to join a road just past Sminhay Farm (see map).

Turn right here and continue for a few hundred yards or so and then cross a gate into a field on your right hand side. Although this is a footpath (see map) no signposts are erected and great care must be taken here to follow the route as in the map. Keep the coppice in front of you to the left hand side and walk on past Harpers Barn to Northay Farm and then through the field to Gunners Hay Farm and from there back to road and on to Peters Gore.

Note: This is a lovely walk on a clear day. The Marshwood Vale is very beautiful. It is, however, very isolated and it is possible to do the entire walk without seeing another person. The paths are sometimes difficult to follow so the 1.25000 Ordnance Map is essential and a hand compass would be useful although the towering mass of Lamberts Castle is a very useful landmark.

Places of interest on walk

Lamberts Castle: Early iron-age fort (2000 B.C.). The walls can still be traced.

Refreshments: None obtainable anywhere. Essential to take your own but there are many suitable spots for a picnic.

Central Dorset

THIS is a region of quiet contentment. Small streams meander through rich meadows and gentle hills invite the walker to explore. The population is sparse and widely spread and many villages do not even boast an inn. The towns Bere Regis and Blandford are small market towns both packed with history and architectural beauty. The walking is gentle but full of beauty and peace.

WALK 13

Valley of the Winterbournes

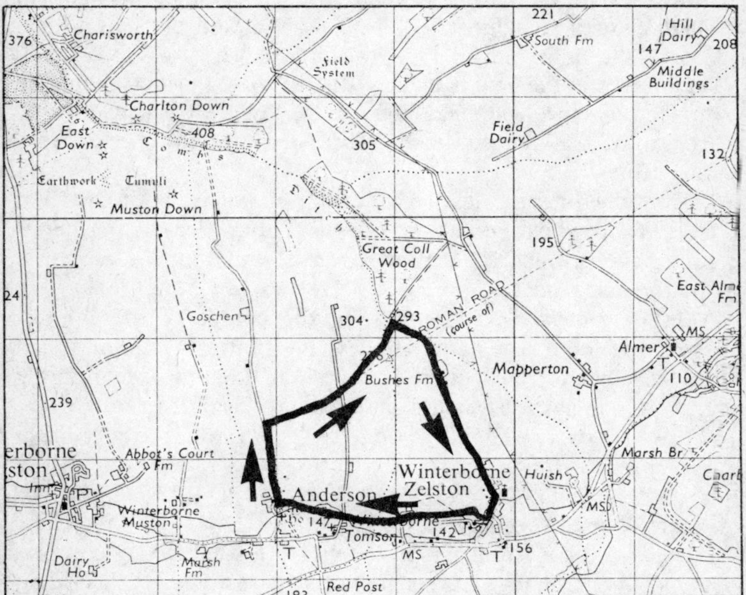

Crown Copyright

Scale: 1 inch = 1 mile

Distance: 5 miles.
Walking time: 2½ hours.
Degree of difficulty: Easy walking but involves some crossing of ploughed fields. Not recommended in wet weather.
Ordnance map: SY 89/99.
Starting point: Church at Winterbourne Zelston. Map ref. 89.9/97.7.

A FEW yards up the hill past the church is a turning to the left and at the end of the lane you will see a stile with a yellow marker on it. Cross the stile and follow the path across the fields over a series of stiles all marked with a yellow spot.

When you reach the turning off to Winterbourne Tomson do make the little detour to visit the church, return and continue on until you reach the turning to Winterbourne Anderson which has a beautiful manor house.

At this point there is a wide lane. Turn right here and walk gently uphill for about a mile. Just past some ruined farm buildings is a small cross roads. Take the path through a farm gate to the right and follow across a field which goes downhill. At the foot of the field is a gate, usually locked, which should be climbed. In the next field you can follow very easily the old Roman road which ran from Dorchester to Shapwick and Badbury Rings.

Continue bearing slightly left until you reach the tip of Great Coll Wood which can easily be seen. From here the path goes south-east to Bushes Farm and then downhill to Winterbourne Zelston and your car.

Note: A pleasant walk, following the course of the Winterbourne which as the name implies only runs in winter and then up into the heart of utterly unspoilt undulating rich farming country and along the course of the old roads of England.

Refreshments: None obtainable on walk. Necessary to take one's own.

Places of interest on route:

Winterbourne Zelston: Small hamlet with some pretty cottages along the stream. Church mercilessly restored in Victorian times.

Winterbourne Tomson: A remote hamlet. So remote that the lovely old church was overlooked by the Victorian restorers, being used as a barn at the time. Treves found it completely deserted in 1906 with broken windows and birds nesting in the pews. Hardy loved this place and left some of his manuscripts to be sold for the restoration so that today it is a thing of unique beauty.

Winterbourne Anderson: One of the loveliest Manor Houses in Dorset built by John Tregonwell of Milton Abbey in 1620. It can best be seen from behind the church. The brick work has a lovely soft texture with every third course of flared bricks burnt to a dark pulple. The gardens are superb in all seasons.

Up Sydling

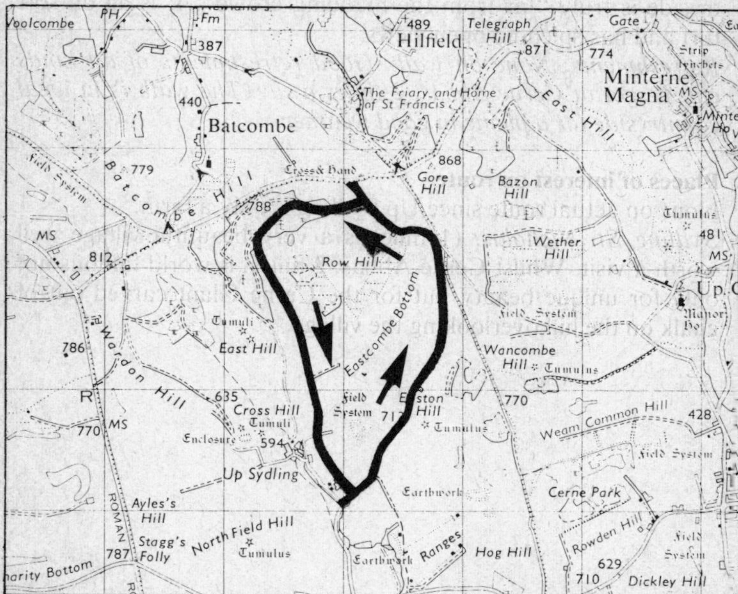

Crown Copyright

Scale: 1 inch = 1 mile

Distance: 5 miles.
Time: 2½ hours.
Degree of difficulty: Easy walking. Not recommended in muddy weather.
Ordnance map: Cerne Abbas. ST 60. 1.25000.
Starting point: The Ford at entrance to Up Sydling. Map ref. 01/63. The car can be parked by the roadside here.

IMMEDIATELY over the ford to the right hand side is a clearly defined path leading up the hill. The path rises some four hundred feet but it is not too steep and is pleasant walking if taken slowly with beautiful views over rolling hills and deep valleys.

When the summit is reached continue along the path shown until you reach the main road. Turn left here for 1000 yards. There is a footpath on your left. Follow the path all the way back to Sydling.

Note: This very lovely walk in the beautiful but remote countryside is truly "far from the madding crowd". It is all on soft turf and has splendid open views.

Refreshments: None on walk. Good refreshments of all kinds can be got at Cerne Abbas, 2 miles away. The walk is in ideal countryside for a picnic in good weather.

Places of interest on route.

None on actual route since Up Sydling is only a farm.

Sydling St. Nicholas: (1 mile) is a very beautiful village well worth a visit. Whilst Cerne Abbas, 2 miles, is world famous not only for unique beauty but for the Cerne Giant carved out of chalk on the hill overlooking the village.

WALK 15

Durweston

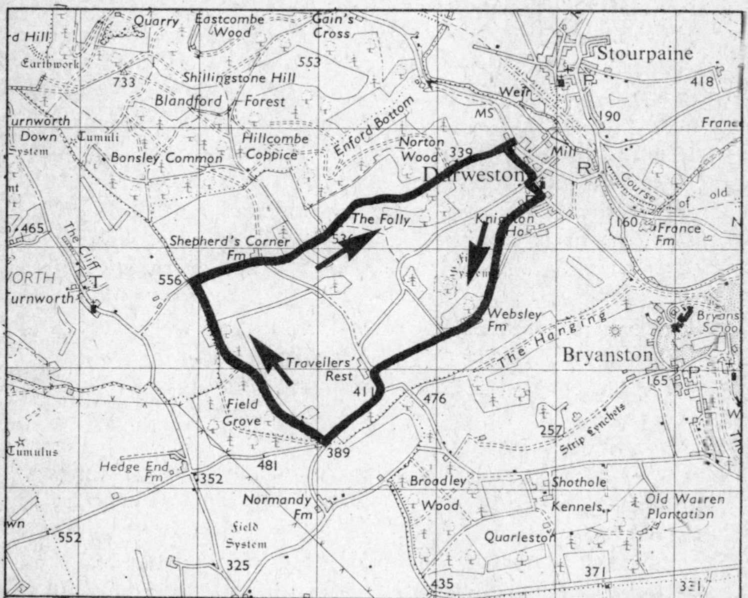

Crown Copyright

Scale: 1 inch = 1 mile

Shepherds Corner, Durweston

Distance: 5 miles.
Walking time: About 2 hours.
Degree of difficulty: Very easy walking.
Ordnance map: Blandford Forum. ST.80. 1.25000.
Starting Point: Durweston. Map ref. 85.8/08.7.

LEAVE the car near the church and continue on until you reach the Post Office on your right hand side. The path is immediately to one side. Continue until you meet another path. When the two join continue on as far as Websley Farm.

The path from here is wide and clear until you reach a

triangle of grass at a T junction. This is Travellers Rest. Turn left here until after about 100 yards you meet another T junction. Take the path to the right and carry on as far as the point where the wood meets the path.

Your path here is right through the wood and out the other side until you meet a path at right angles. The distance of this section is a mile and a half.

At the intersection turn right and continue in a straight line past Shepherds Corner Farm and on up the hill. Soon afterwards you will see a track to the left up into the Forest. A little further on the right hand side there are some farm buildings and immediately beyond the path continues through the field and on through the wood and thence downhill direct to Durweston. Turn right at main road and walk back through the village to your car.

Note: A very pleasant easy walk through quiet remote countryside.

Refreshments: None in Durweston or on route. Good snacks at Shillingstone, 2 miles, at the Seymer Arms or in Blandford where there are several good hotels and restaurants.

Places of interest on route.

Durweston: A charming hamlet with some attractive houses. The church, a typical downland flint building is worth a visit although much restored. Over the inside of the entrance door is a remarkable carving of St. Eloy the patron saint of blacksmiths. This hamlet is mentioned in the Doomsday Book as a site of vineyards.

WALK 16

Bere Regis

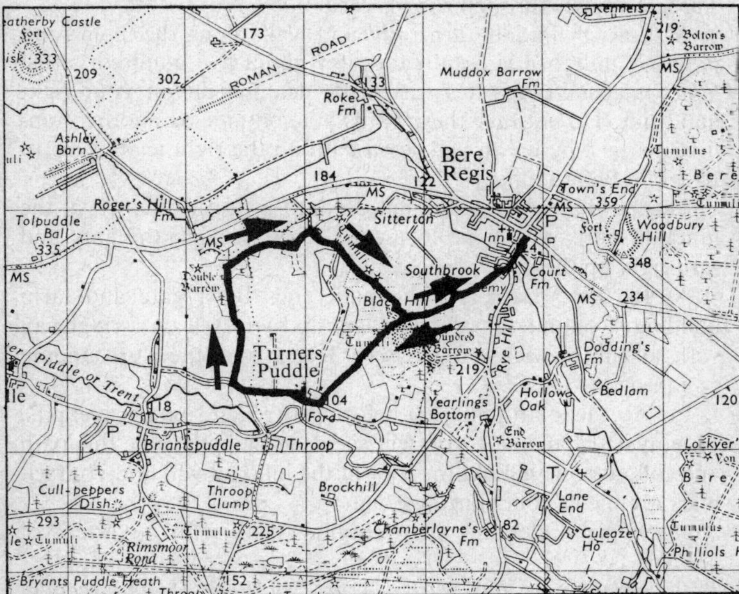

Crown Copyright Scale: 1 inch = 1 mile

Turners Puddle, Bere Regis

Distance: 5 miles.
Walking time: 2½ hours approximately.
Degree of difficulty: Easy walking.
Ordnance map: Bere Regis SY 89/99.
Starting point: Bere Regis. Map Ref. 94.7/84.8.

PARK your car in Bere Regis. The "Royal Oak" has a good car park. Start from the Royal Oak and walk down the road towards Bovington and Wool for about 200 yards. At the bend you will see a turning, "Southbrook". Turn right here and follow the road through council houses. After the first bend you will see a path by the side of the cemetery leading up into the woods.

Follow this path until you come to a wood. Here you must be careful not to take the path up hill to the right or keep to the edge of the forest on the left. Keep to the middle of the wood until you reach a path going at right angles. Follow this to Damer Hill and then take the turning to the left which leads downhill to Turners Puddle through a farm yard.

At Turners Puddle turn right and walk along the main road past the church and continue on for about five hundred yards. You will pass two gates with paths leading off on your right hand side. Do not take these paths but continue on another hundred yards where you will see a path on the right leading up to Kite Hill Plantation.

This path is well marked but do not turn off to the left at the junction until you come to a gate. Pass through the gate and turn right up the hill.

At the top of the hill the path goes by a gate and farm building. Continue on and you will find yourself on a ridgeway with beautiful views over Bere Regis and the surrounding countryside.

Follow this path until just before you reach some gravel pits, on your left hand side you will see a bridle path, take this path and follow downhill. At the foot of the hill you will find yourself back almost at your starting point.

Note: A very pleasant easy country walk with a variety of scenery.

Refreshments: At the "Drax Arms" in Bere Regis excellent snacks are obtainable. Snacks are also obtainable at the "Royal Oak", and teas can be obtained in the village.

Places of interest on route:

Bere Regis: Rather drab village with a beautiful church which has one of the finest roofs in England. Not to be missed. Also one mile to the east is Woodbury Hill, an Iron-Age fort and scene for many centuries of the largest fair in the south of England.

Turners Puddle: A remote hamlet with little else than the church and rectory in "venerable companionship" as Treves comments. The church once in ruins is now restored. There is a little Norman font decorated with interlacing arches and nail head ornament.

North Dorset

NORTH Dorset has a charm of its own. It is a very fertile region of rich farms, gentle hills, smiling plains, sparsely populated with small villages and hamlets. It is a region of great antiquity and steeped in history, with the three towns of Sherborne, Shaftesbury and Sturminster Newton. Sherborne, is one of the most historic towns in England, Shaftesbury is the highest town of any size in England and Sturminster Newton is an interesting market town, all are of great beauty and packed with history. This is a region beloved of the Saxons and they have left their imprint on all sides. Walking is easy because the hills are rolling but the countryside is varied and the walks are very satisfying.

Sturminster Newton

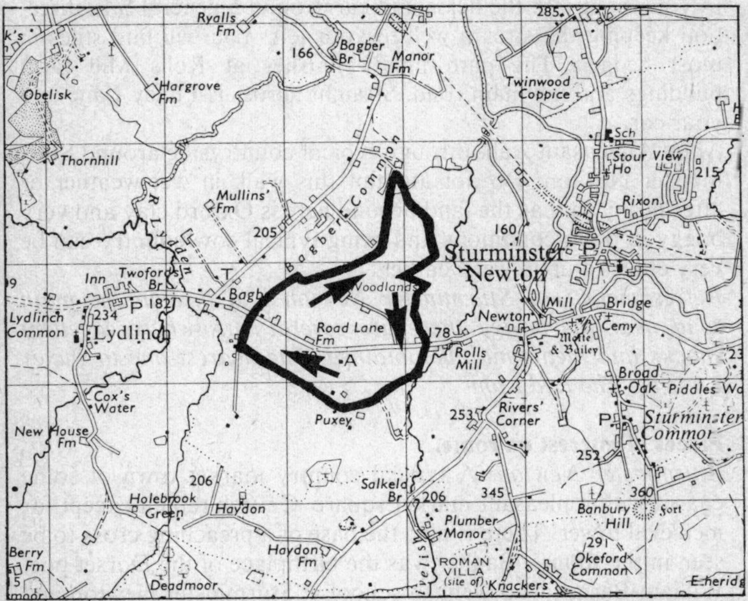

Crown Copyright Scale: 1 inch = 1 mile

Sturminster Newton, Puxey, Bagber, Sturminster Newton

Distance: 5 miles.
Walking time: 2½ hours.
Degree of difficulty: Easy Walking.
Ordnance map: Sturminster Newton ST.71.
Starting point: Puxey Lane. ½ mile due west from Sturminster Newton bridge on the A357, Map ref. 77.2/13.3.

LEAVE the car at first convenient point in Puxey Lane. Follow the road down for about a thousand yards. Turn right at junction and continue on until you reach the T junction with a farm straight ahead. Turn right here and continue on until you reach the main road. Cross over and continue on up the lane. At the T junction follow the path to the right but almost immediately around the curve keep to the path going straight on, do not turn right up to the farm.

The path is very well defined now until you reach the farm buildings at Pleak House Farm. At this point cross the first gate to your right into the fields and carry on in a general S.E. direction keeping the stream well to your left. You will find stiles in most hedges. The path finally finishes at Rolls Mill farm buildings and the main road. Straight across is Puxey Lane and your car.

Note: A pleasant walk through typical countryside around Sturminster Newton. Do not attempt this walk in wet weather or after heavy rain as the land around here is Oxford clay and very boggy in these conditions and being typical cow country can be very churned up in wet weather.

Refreshments: In Sturminster Newton and also in the main road near the bridge there are several inns where excellent snacks and meals may be obtained. The nearest one to Puxey Lane is "The Red Lion".

Places of interest on route.

Sturminster Newton: A typical country market town of some charm with a pleasant market square. Church rebuilt except for medieval tower. There is also the base of a preaching cross to be seen in the square. Bagber was the birthplace of the Dorset poet William Barnes who went to school at Sturminster Newton and here he wrote some of his finest poems. The bridge over the river must be one of the most photographed bridges in England.

Rockbourne

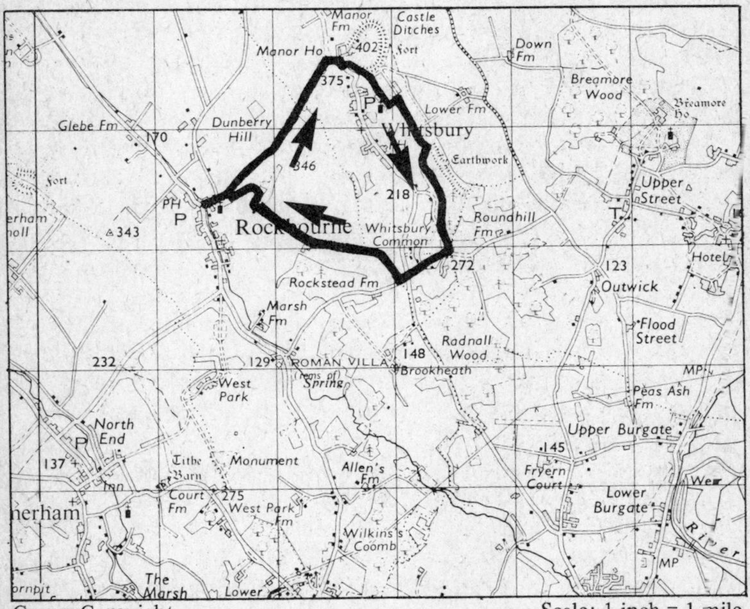

Crown Copyright Scale: 1 inch = 1 mile

Rockbourne, Castle Ditches, Rockbourne

Distance: 5 miles.
Walking time: 2 hours.
Degree of difficulty: Very easy walking.
Ordnance map: Fordingbridge. SU11. 1.25000.
Starting point: Rockbourne village. Map ref. 18.2/11.4.

THERE is a good car park behind the "Rose and Thistle" in centre of village.

Take the turning from the main road up to the church and Manor Farm. Keep to the left and you will see a grass path leading to a gate marked "Bridle Path". Continue on and follow clearly marked path through several gates until you reach the Racing Stables with horses in paddocks to either side of your path.

The road follows slightly right past the Manor House and then almost immediately you will see a sign post "To Church". Follow along this path which leaves the iron-age fort on your left hand side. Ahead of you is a narrow path to the church.

Follow this until you see a large bungalow the other side of a field. A path leads to this where you will turn right and follow the path through Whitsbury Wood keeping well to right hand side. This path leads on to the main road. Follow down hill past a large Neo-Georgian house on your left. A little further on is a cross roads. Take the road to the right and then turn right up a track which leads to a farm yard. Cross right through this and along the path on the other side until you reach a stile on your left hand side. Cross the stile and go down hill to Manor Farm and the church.

No Strictly speaking this walk should not be included in a book of Dorset Walks since most of it is just over the Hampshire border. It is, however, a charming walk for people living in north-west Dorset and as such thought to be worthy of inclusion. A charming easy walk.

Refreshments: Excellent meals and snacks obtainable at "Rose and Thistle" inn in centre of Rockbourne village.

Places of interest on route.

Rockbourne: Very beautiful village with many charming houses set in gardens of great beauty. The thirteenth century church is beautifully sited and worth a visit. Note monastic remains in neighbouring farm house buildings.

Castle Ditches: Early iron-age fortification. Multi-vallate.

Roman Villa: Signposted in Rockbourne village. About 1 mile to the south-east. Open Good Friday to end of September. Remarkable excavation and museum. Should not be missed.

Sherborne

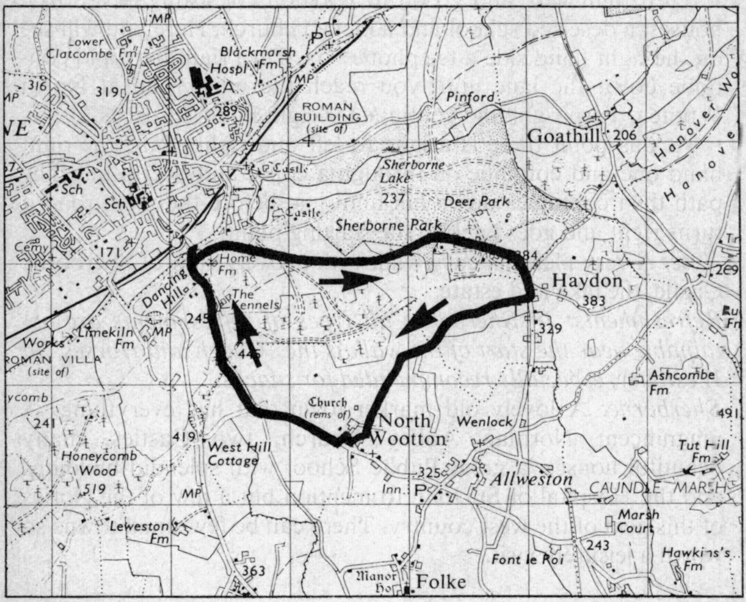

Crown Copyright

Scale: 1 inch = 1 mile

Distance: 6 miles.
Walking time: 3 hours.
Degree of difficulty: Very easy walking.
Ordnance map: Sherborne ST61. 1.25000.
Starting point: Entrance gates to New Castle.

JUST outside the gates of the New Castle you will see a path leading up a steep bank. Follow this path alongside the fence all the way. After a few hundred yards you will find the path diverges. Keep to the left hand one.

This path passes right in front of the Castle and lake and then continues up-hill past a lodge. At the summit the path goes on for a short while until you reach a gateway.

Passing through the gateway follow the path to the right until you reach a point near the old camp where the road diverges. Here again take the left hand one and continue on until you reach a road.

Turn right here and go on to Haydon consisting of a dozen houses, a deserted school and a locked church. Here you will see on the right hand side a telephone box. Turn right here and continue down the lane until you reach the main road at North Wooten. Turn right and continue for eight hundred yards.

At this point there is a lane to left and right. Take the right hand one and continue on through a copse and over a hill. The path then continues down hill until just before the main road it turns right and goes back to the starting point.

Note: A very pleasant easy walk with a lovely view of Sherborne Castle, the lake and estate.

Refreshments: In Sherborne all types of refreshments are obtainable near the start of the walk is the "Coach and Horses" at Westbury, especially recommended for snacks.

Sherborne: A lovely old market town that has everything. A magnificent Norman Abbey Church, two Castles, many beautiful houses, a great Public School with splendid buildings and the Hospital of St. John to mention but a few of the glories of this gem of the west country. There can be few small towns so worth a leisurely visit.

Shaftesbury

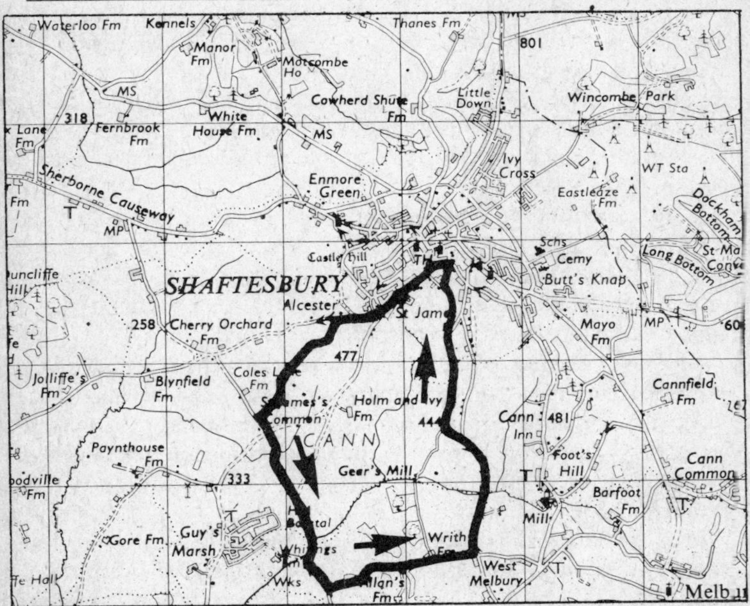

Crown Copyright

Scale: 1 inch = 1 mi e

Blackmoor Vale, Shaftesbury

Distance: 5 miles.
Time: About 2½ hours.
Degree of difficulty: Mildly strenuous.
Ordnance map: Shaftesbury ST82. 1.25000.
Starting point: Entrance to Shaftesbury Abbey. Leave car in central town car park.

FROM the Abbey gateway continue along until you see a path going downhill. At the foot of the hill continue on to the right until you reach a junction. Here you will see a signpost to "Stour Row".

Follow this road for a short distance. On your right hand side is a road. 70 yards past this on the left hand side there is a path across the field in a south west direction. The path ends at a roadway where you should turn left to cross roads just ahead.

Here straight ahead is a gateway, climb and cross fields until you see a road in front. Here you can either turn right and go through the fields to Whitney Farm or follow the road since both paths meet at the farm. The choice should depend on the weather as the ground is very marshy in wet weather.

Continue along the road past the farm and uphill for a few hundred yards and then take the left fork at the road junction. Follow this road past Writh Farm as far as the cross-roads at Cornhill Cottage.

Turn left here and go down French Mill Lane and past the mill at foot of hill. A few hundred yards further on there is a road junction, take the left fork and continue on past Holyrood Farm until you reach a signpost. Take the road to the left here, and not the one marked Shaftesbury.

Follow this lane around until you reach on the right hand side "Gold Hill". Turn here and climb up what must be one of the loveliest streets in England and certainly the most photographed. The great wall of the Abbey on the one side and the beautiful houses on the other dropping sharply into the Blackmoor Vale make this a scene of near perfection.

Note: Although this walk has rather more road walking than usual these roads are little frequented and make pleasant walking. The climb back to Shaftesbury is, of necessity, rather steep but if taken slowly presents no difficulty.

Refreshments: Excellent snacks at "Mitre Inn" in High Street near entrance to Abbey walk.

On the return a very good tea or evening meal can be obtained at "King Alfred's Kitchen" also near entrance to Abbey.

Places of interest on route:

Shaftesbury: A superb Saxon hill top town, the highest in England overlooking the beautiful fertile Blackmoor Vale. Full of lovely old houses and drenched in history. Once site of largest Nunnery in England. The Abbey which should not be missed is open from Easter to end of September every day except Monday. There is also an excellent small museum which should be visited if time permits.